HEY YOU

My name is Victoria, consider me a friend that you can tell all your secrets, and feelings without anyone ever knowing. I am here to walk you through this process. Yes, I know you're asking yourself, "What is the process, and why do I have to do it?" This book was written with you in mind. Yes, you! This book will help you to improve in not only how you see the world, but how you see yourself as well. So, I'm asking you to commit to this journey. I will be here to guide you the whole way through. Haha and I promise not to make you read on every page, but you will need a pencil. So, what do you say? Sign your name down below, if the answer is yes.

____

STEP 1

Do you know what an identity is? If you were to Google for the definition, you would find that it means what or who a person or thing is. In this case, we are focusing on you. Who are you? When I ask that question, what comes to mind? For most people, we tend to think, "I am a student," "I am a basketball player," or" I am a son or daughter". You can and might be all those things, but I want to know who you are. When the season changes and school is out for the summer, who are you?

I want to tell you a secret about me. If you were to ask me this question a few years ago, I wouldn't have an answer. My goal is that you will start the journey of discovering your identity. I don't want you to spend years being confused like I was.

Here in this workbook, we will have fun doing activities together. This journey will also teach you how to treat yourself and others. Putting in the work is vital, but this process only works if you stay committed to what you learn. Do you want to feel loved and chosen? Would you like to feel seen and understood; of course you do. We all want to feel included, with a sense that we belong.

It is a difficult task to know where you belong if you don't know who you are. For example, if you were a band member spending all your time in the gym, you would feel out of place. You miss out on the chance to play with all the other band members. Let's work together to ensure you won't miss out on the fun of life because you are in the wrong place.

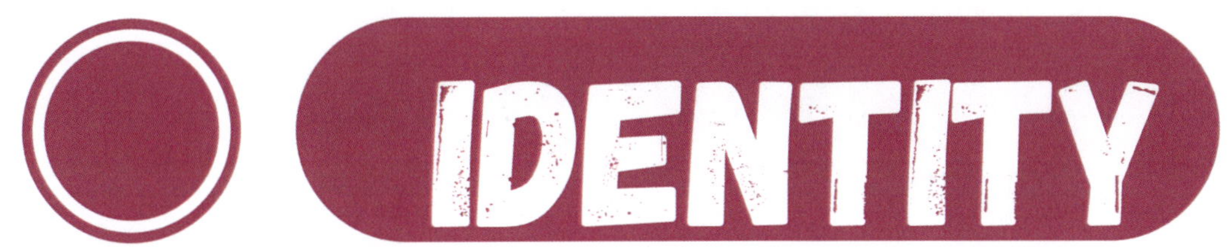

Do you know what an identity is? If you were to Google for the definition, you would find that it means what or who a person or thing is. In this case, we are focusing on you. Who are you? When I ask that question, what comes to mind? For most people, we tend to think, "I am a student," "I am a basketball player," or" I am a son or daughter". You can and might be all those things, but I want to know who you are. When the season changes and school is out for the summer, who are you?

I want to tell you a secret about me. If you were to ask me this question a few years ago, I wouldn't have an answer. My goal is that you will start the journey of discovering your identity. I don't want you to spend years being confused like I was.

Here in this workbook, we will have fun doing activities together. This journey will also teach you how to treat yourself and others. Putting in the work is vital, but this process only works if you stay committed to what you learn. Do you want to feel loved and chosen? Would you like to feel seen and understood; of course you do. We all want to feel included, with a sense that we belong.

It is a difficult task to know where you belong if you don't know who you are. For example, if you were a band member spending all your time in the gym, you would feel out of place. You miss out on the chance to play with all the other band members. Let's work together to ensure you won't miss out on the fun of life because you are in the wrong place.

Having an identity helped me to choose better friendships and to make decisions that would be good for me. I know now I deserve to be loved, supported, and protected. Do you pick friends that walk away from drama and treat you kindly? Do you say yes to situations that make you uncomfortable to make others happy? These are a few ways to tell if you know who you are and how you should be treated.

There is always room for improvement, so if you're doing good with identity, that's great. We will dive a little deeper soon.

REJECTION

Rejection can make anyone feel alone and hurt. We can all feel rejected by anyone in our lives, even strangers that we barely know. Having a crush who doesn't like us back can cause rejection. Being rejected can spark in our minds the belief that we are not good enough. Busy parents who don't make it to important events like our sports and award days can leave behind rejection in our hearts. Even wanting to be friends with the wrong people can hurt when they decide they don't want to be friends to you.

Has any of these situations ever happened to you? It's likely because these scenarios happen every day. Did you take it personally when no one chose you? Some change their appearance to change the minds of others, some quit playing sports, and some isolate themselves due to rejection. No one can stop these situations and others like it from happening, but we can work together to create positive ways of handling them.

When it's time to celebrate, we want to share the moment with our loved ones. Yet, sometimes those we love can't or won't show up when we want them to. It may be when your mom doesn't show up to see you perform at school because of her work schedule. It may be that your Dad is busy with other plans, but both can bring sadness. Does that mean you stop excelling at school, no. You don't stop because of a lack of support ever. You continue to do what you love for yourself. If what you're putting your time into brings you joy, then you don't give up.

Do you remember the last time you said, "So, I don't care," when someone hurt your feelings? We both know that deep down you cared a little, so here we will learn to use rejection as redirection. When they say they don't want to sit with you at lunch, then you can smile. Do you know why? Because if they leave the seat open next to you, now someone who is kind has the opportunity to sit there. It's all about perspective. During our time together we will work on your perspective because our goal is for you to be what.... HAPPY.

LOW
SELF-
ESTEEM

Do you have a favorite person in the whole wide world? Is your favorite person near you right now in this moment? They should be super close to you because you should be your favorite person. You should be able to look in the mirror and love what you see. You should be able to enjoy being with yourself. Simply knowing in your mind that you're supposed to like yourself won't be enough.

There was a time in my life that I didn't like myself very much. I didn't feel like the amazing person I am today. Are you fun, cool, friendly, and nice to others? If you aren't that's okay, we will work on it, but if you are that's great. Being nice to those around us is a great thing to do. Say it with me treat others the way you want to be treated! YES, but I am more concerned with how you treat yourself. Are you speaking to yourself with love and respect? You may say nice things to your friends so they feel good, but what are the words you whisper to yourself? No need to answer now just think about it.

The plan here is to boost your level of self-esteem. When we don't have high self-esteem we suffer especially from things like depression and anxiety.

Depression can ruin many days or even years of your life with the feeling of sadness, lack of energy, and even being hard on yourself. Anxiety can show up in your life making it hard to focus, trouble sleeping, and anger to name a few. I found myself struggling with both, but today I am free from depression and living anxiety-free. If you feel like you're experiencing this, I'm here to tell you there is hope. All you have to do is stay committed to the process. It is possible to be beautiful, smart, and an important person, but you never know it. I'm here to show you how awesome you are. What good is it to have it all and still not see it in yourself?

EXHAUSTED

Looking at the clock and a list of what needs to be done can be overwhelming. Have you ever felt like there weren't enough minutes in a day to complete everything you need to do? Being a student, a child, and for some, a sibling can add a lot of pressure. Being in school there are expectations set for you by your parents, family, teachers, and your coaches. It is fine if you struggle a little with managing all the requirements. Our goal is not to remove the goals set before you but to help you manage them in a healthy way.

School comes with a checklist, and your home life might have one as well. Keeping up with your chores takes energy, as well as spending time with your family. You might have younger siblings that you help your parents with also. What is your home life like? When you get home do you have a lot of free time to yourself to relax and have fun? If you answered no, then what are you busy doing? Helping your family and friends is a great thing to do, but you have to help yourself first. We will work together to help you manage all of your expectations.

The hardest part of having many expectations of you is the desire to complete them all. It never feels good to disappoint the ones we love, but what about you? We went over in the last chapter that you have to love yourself! You should be your favorite person. So some great exercises to help balance your life are:
Take breaks when you need them.
Focus on one task at a time.
Speaking up when you feel tired.
Asking for help, when you need it.
Never say "yes", when you want to say "no".

Following the steps above will make it easy for you to create boundaries.

Example:

I will not work on anything during my break time, but I will help those I love.

I will only work on one thing at a time, but I won't stress over a lot at once.

I will speak up for myself and be friends with people who respect my needs.

I will not overwork my mind to make others happy.

I will make decisions that I can be proud of.

Perfect! Keep these affirmations in mind for later.

MISTREATED

Some people say words don't hurt, but that isn't true. Words have the power to cause deep pain when used as a weapon. Pop quiz! Think of a time when someone said something negative to or about you. It's easy to remember even if it happened a long time ago. Do you know why? The answer is that words are powerful.

Perfect, now switch gears. If someone you know asked the same question, would they think of a time when your words hurt them?

Words just like touch can violate others when used as a weapon. Being touched in any way that makes you uncomfortable or causes you pain is a violation. Unfortunately, there can be a lack of trust because of inappropriate touch. If inappropriate touch has happened to you or someone close to you, finish out this chapter. Now, if this doesn't apply to you, you are ready for step 2. If this is a part of your story, you have my sympathy. Now that you have it, I pray you trade it something better. I recommend trading sympathy for freedom. The important thing about freedom is that it releases you from shame, guilt, nightmares, and pain.

As a child I experienced beings violated , so I know it's hard not to be angery or upset with your self. So take a deep breath and start step 2 when you are ready.

I know you know your experiences, everything you've been through. But I'm curious to know...

How Well Do You Know Yourself?

WE ALL HAVE THINGS WE DON'T LIKE ABOUT OURSELVES.
IN THE BUBBLES WRITE DOWN A FEW THINGS YOU DON'T LIKE ABOUT YOU

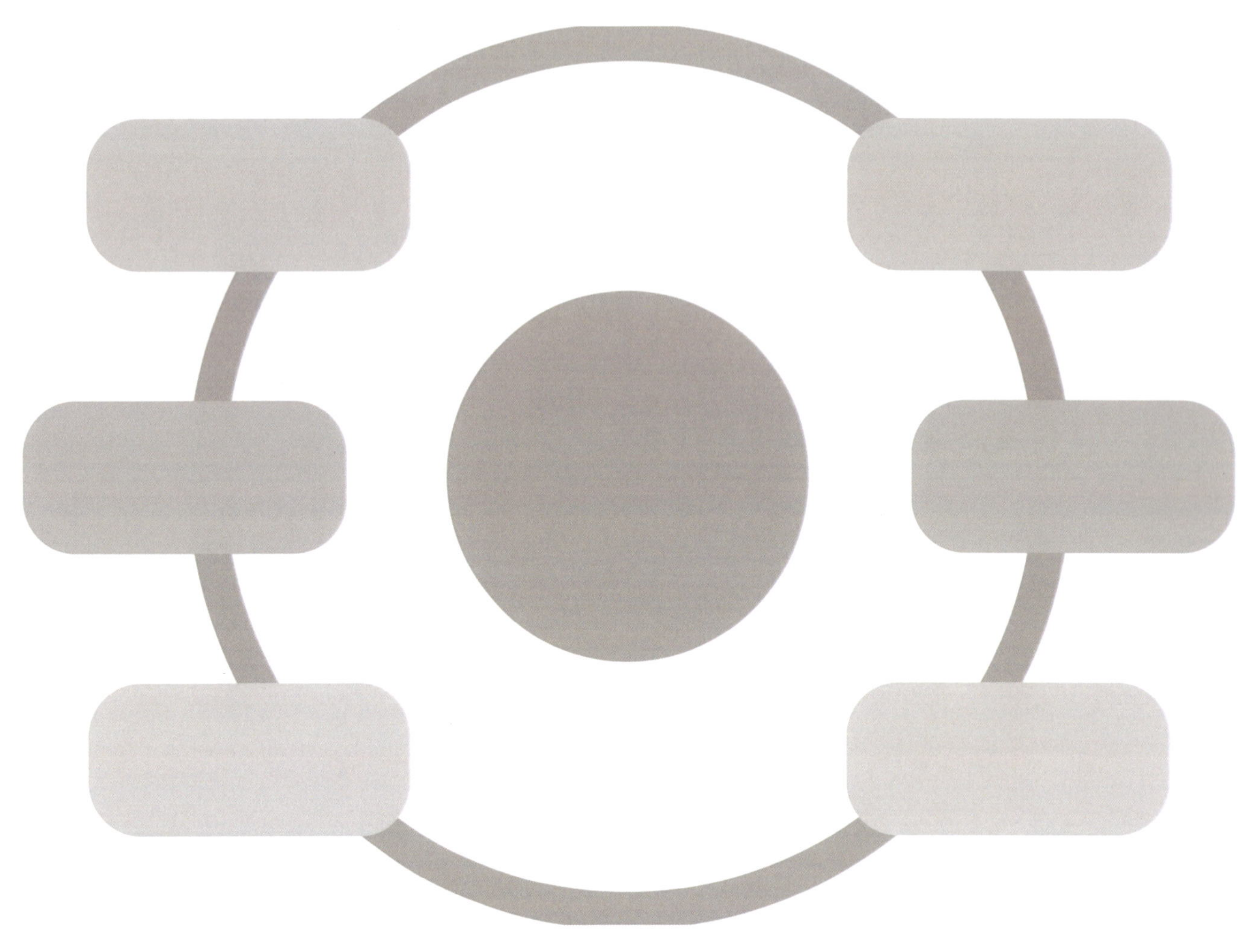

NOW WE ARE GOING TO TRY SOMETHING A LITTLE HARDER.

CAN YOU LIST DOWN BELOW 6 THINGS YOU LOVE ABOUT YOURSELF?

NOW JUST BETWEEN YOU AND I. WHICH PART WAS EASIER TO FILL OUT? IF THE POSITIVE SIDE WAS HARDER FOR YOU, IT'S OKAY! THIS IS ONLY THE BEGINNING. WE ARE JUST GETTING STARTED.

LOOK AT YOU

You did it! I know it may not feel like much, but I'm so proud of you. You didn't quit. You were honest with yourself, and you're doing the work.
You could've stopped and given up already. I promise you are stronger than you think you are, and you will feel even better once you complete this journey.

REMEMBER TO PACE YOURSELF. IT'S ALL ABOUT YOU AND YOUR JOURNEY. THERE'S NO TIME LIMIT AND THERE'S NO RIGHT OR WRONG WAY. NO PRESSURE!

YOU SAID SOME NEGATIVE STUFF ABOUT HOW YOU FEEL ABOUT YOURSELF.
GO BACK AND READ WHAT YOU WROTE DOWN BEFORE.

LET'S DIVE DEEPER!

ON THE LEFT WRITE DOWN THE NEGATIVE THINGS YOU SAID. ON THE RIGHT WRITE DOWN THE NAME OF EVERY PERSON WHO SAID THAT NEGATIVE THING TO YOU.

Example

I am not pretty → Mom Jamie David

Now it's your turn..

③ LET'S DIVE DEEPER!

ON THE LEFT WRITE DOWN THE NEGATIVE THINGS YOU SAID. ON THE RIGHT WRITE DOWN THE NAME OF EVERY PERSON WHO SAID THAT NEGATIVE THING TO YOU.

Example

I am not pretty → Mom Jamie David

MORE ???

MORE ???

MORE ???

THE WORDS THAT ARE SPOKEN TO US CAN STICK WITH US FOR A LONG TIME. WHEN NEGATIVE WORDS ARE SPOKEN WE USUALLY REPLAY THEM IN OUR MINDS.

THIS PAGE IS DEDICATED TO ONLY ONE NEGATIVE CHARACTERISTIC. WRITE IN EACH BUBBLE THE NAME OF THE PERSON WHO SAID IT. TELL ME EXACTLY HOW THEY SAID IT AND HOW IT MADE YOU FEEL.

NEAGATIVE FEELING:

Not pretty/ handsome enough

What were you told?

#1 My sister she sad she's the cute one, and I'm the smart one. It made me wish I liked more like her. I wish I was beautiful too.

#2

#3

WAIT THERE'S MORE

ARE YOU READY ?.... THIS PART IS SUPER IMPORTANT. IT'S TIME TO LET GO. I KNOW THE THINGS YOU SHARED ON THE PREVIOUS PAGE HURT YOU. I ENCOURAGE YOU TO LEAVE IT HERE. THIS JOURNEY IS ALL ABOUT YOU AND YOU WILL FEEL SO MUCH BETTER AFTER YOU DO THIS.

NEAGATIVE FEELING:

____

THE WORDS THAT ARE SPOKEN TO US CAN STICK WITH US FOR A LONG TIME. WHEN NEGATIVE WORDS ARE SPOKEN WE USUALLY REPLAY THEM IN OUR MINDS.

THIS PAGE IS DEDICATED TO ONLY ONE NEGATIVE CHARACTERISTIC. WRITE IN EACH BUBBLE THE NAME OF THE PERSON WHO SAID IT. TELL ME EXACTLY HOW THEY SAID IT AND HOW IT MADE YOU FEEL.

NEAGATIVE FEELING:

What were you told?

#1

#2

#3

WAIT THERE'S MORE

ARE YOU READY ?.... THIS PART IS SUPER IMPORTANT. IT'S TIME TO LET GO. I KNOW THE THINGS YOU SHARED ON THE PREVIOUS PAGE HURT YOU. I ENCOURAGE YOU TO LEAVE IT HERE. THIS JOURNEY IS ALL ABOUT YOU AND YOU WILL FEEL SO MUCH BETTER AFTER YOU DO THIS.

NEAGATIVE FEELING:

____

③ THE WORDS THAT ARE SPOKEN TO US CAN STICK WITH US FOR A LONG TIME. WHEN NEGATIVE WORDS ARE SPOKEN WE USUALLY REPLAY THEM IN OUR MINDS.

THIS PAGE IS DEDICATED TO ONLY ONE NEGATIVE CHARACTERISTIC. WRITE IN EACH BUBBLE THE NAME OF THE PERSON WHO SAID IT. TELL ME EXACTLY HOW THEY SAID IT AND HOW IT MADE YOU FEEL.

NEAGATIVE FEELING:

What were you told?

#1

#2

#3

WAIT THERE'S MORE

ARE YOU READY ?.... THIS PART IS SUPER IMPORTANT. IT'S TIME TO LET GO. I KNOW THE THINGS YOU SHARED ON THE PREVIOUS PAGE HURT YOU. I ENCOURAGE YOU TO LEAVE IT HERE. THIS JOURNEY IS ALL ABOUT YOU AND YOU WILL FEEL SO MUCH BETTER AFTER YOU DO THIS.

NEAGATIVE FEELING:

____

THE WORDS THAT ARE SPOKEN TO US CAN STICK WITH US FOR A LONG TIME. WHEN NEGATIVE WORDS ARE SPOKEN WE USUALLY REPLAY THEM IN OUR MINDS.

THIS PAGE IS DEDICATED TO ONLY ONE NEGATIVE CHARACTERISTIC. WRITE IN EACH BUBBLE THE NAME OF THE PERSON WHO SAID IT. TELL ME EXACTLY HOW THEY SAID IT AND HOW IT MADE YOU FEEL.

NEAGATIVE FEELING:

What were you told?

#1

#2

#3

Do you believe them?

● YES
or
● NO

Where are you now ?

● I forgive

● Im want to forgive

● Not ready to forgive yet

WAIT THERE'S MORE

ARE YOU READY ?.... THIS PART IS SUPER IMPORTANT. IT'S TIME TO LET GO. I KNOW THE THINGS YOU SHARED ON THE PREVIOUS PAGE HURT YOU. I ENCOURAGE YOU TO LEAVE IT HERE. THIS JOURNEY IS ALL ABOUT YOU AND YOU WILL FEEL SO MUCH BETTER AFTER YOU DO THIS.

NEAGATIVE FEELING:

____

THE WORDS THAT ARE SPOKEN TO US CAN STICK WITH US FOR A LONG TIME. WHEN NEGATIVE WORDS ARE SPOKEN WE USUALLY REPLAY THEM IN OUR MINDS.

THIS PAGE IS DEDICATED TO ONLY ONE NEGATIVE CHARACTERISTIC. WRITE IN EACH BUBBLE THE NAME OF THE PERSON WHO SAID IT. TELL ME EXACTLY HOW THEY SAID IT AND HOW IT MADE YOU FEEL.

NEAGATIVE FEELING:

What were you told?

#1

#2

#3

WAIT THERE'S MORE

ARE YOU READY ?.... THIS PART IS SUPER IMPORTANT. IT'S TIME TO LET GO. I KNOW THE THINGS YOU SHARED ON THE PREVIOUS PAGE HURT YOU. I ENCOURAGE YOU TO LEAVE IT HERE. THIS JOURNEY IS ALL ABOUT YOU AND YOU WILL FEEL SO MUCH BETTER AFTER YOU DO THIS.

NEAGATIVE FEELING:

____

THE WORDS THAT ARE SPOKEN TO US CAN STICK WITH US FOR A LONG TIME. WHEN NEGATIVE WORDS ARE SPOKEN WE USUALLY REPLAY THEM IN OUR MINDS.

THIS PAGE IS DEDICATED TO ONLY ONE NEGATIVE CHARACTERISTIC. WRITE IN EACH BUBBLE THE NAME OF THE PERSON WHO SAID IT. TELL ME EXACTLY HOW THEY SAID IT AND HOW IT MADE YOU FEEL.

NEAGATIVE FEELING:

____

What were you told?

#1

#2

#3

WAIT THERE'S MORE

ARE YOU READY ?.... THIS PART IS SUPER IMPORTANT. IT'S TIME TO LET GO. I KNOW THE THINGS YOU SHARED ON THE PREVIOUS PAGE HURT YOU. I ENCOURAGE YOU TO LEAVE IT HERE. THIS JOURNEY IS ALL ABOUT YOU AND YOU WILL FEEL SO MUCH BETTER AFTER YOU DO THIS.

NEAGATIVE FEELING:

____

THE WORDS THAT ARE SPOKEN TO US CAN STICK WITH US FOR A LONG TIME. WHEN NEGATIVE WORDS ARE SPOKEN WE USUALLY REPLAY THEM IN OUR MINDS.

THIS PAGE IS DEDICATED TO ONLY ONE NEGATIVE CHARACTERISTIC. WRITE IN EACH BUBBLE THE NAME OF THE PERSON WHO SAID IT. TELL ME EXACTLY HOW THEY SAID IT AND HOW IT MADE YOU FEEL.

NEAGATIVE FEELING:

What were you told?

#1

#2

#3

Do you believe them?

● YES

or

● NO

Where are you now ?

● I forgive

● Im want to forgive

● Not ready to forgive yet

WAIT THERE'S MORE

ARE YOU READY ?.... THIS PART IS SUPER IMPORTANT. IT'S TIME TO LET GO. I KNOW THE THINGS YOU SHARED ON THE PREVIOUS PAGE HURT YOU. I ENCOURAGE YOU TO LEAVE IT HERE. THIS JOURNEY IS ALL ABOUT YOU AND YOU WILL FEEL SO MUCH BETTER AFTER YOU DO THIS.

NEAGATIVE FEELING:

____

STEP 4

IT'S
TIME TO
GET
Positive

SHHH... ONLY POSITIVITY

WE ARE OFFICIALLY ON THE POSITIVITY TRAIN. TIME TO SWITCH GEARS. YOU TALKED ABOUT THE PAIN, SADNESS, AND DISAPPOINTMENTS. WHAT ARE THE NICE THINGS YOU THINK ABOUT YOURSELF?

❶ ❷ ❸ ❹ Nice

WHY?

1. I'm always sweet to others.
2.
3.
4.

4 SHHH... ONLY POSITIVITY

WE ARE OFFICIALLY ON THE POSITIVITY TRAIN. TIME TO SWITCH GEARS. YOU TALKED ABOUT THE PAIN, SADNESS, AND DISAPPOINTMENTS. WHAT ARE THE NICE THINGS YOU THINK ABOUT YOURSELF?

WHY?

4 CALL ON YOUR PEOPLE

ASK YOUR CLOSE FRIENDS AND FAMILY WHAT'S SOMETHING THEY LOVE ABOUT YOU.
YOU WOULD BE SURPRISE AT HOW MUCH THOSE WHO LOVE US SEE THINGS THAT WE DON'T SEE IN YOURSELF

WHO?

Sister

CALL ON YOUR PEOPLE

ASK YOUR CLOSE FRIENDS AND FAMILY WHAT'S SOMETHING THEY LOVE ABOUT YOU. YOU WOULD BE SURPRISE AT HOW MUCH THOSE WHO LOVE US SEE THINGS THAT WE DON'T SEE IN YOURSELF

WHO?

STEP 5

Write it!
Say it!!
See it!!!

SAY & SEE

DID YOU KNOW THAT YOUR WORDS HAVE POWER? THINK ON IT FOR A MOMENT. WHEN YOU SPEAK THINGS REPEATEDLY YOU SEE THEM IN YOUR LIFE. FOR EXAMPLE IF YOU CONSTANTLY SAY NEGATIVE THINGS... BOOM NEGATIVITY IS WHAT YOU SEE.

SO PAY ATTENTION BECAUSE I'M GOING TO GIVE YOU A CHEAT CODE FOR LIFE. NO MATTER HOW OLD YOU GET, THE INFORMATION YOU'RE ABOUT TO LEARN WILL ALWAYS BENEFIT YOU.

So take a deep breathe and turn the page, when you're ready.

WHAT TO SAY
Spotlight Words

I am...

Loved	Smart
Special	Kind
Brave	Strong
Chosen	Supported
Protected	Important
Forgiven	Valuable

I'm a...

Leader	Gift
Masterpiece	Friend
Asset	Overcomer

WHAT TO SAY

What would you like to be?

WHERE TO SAY IT

STEP 1: GO TO A MIRROR TO START YOUR DAY

STEP 2: BE THANKFUL FOR WAKING YOU UP

STEP 3: TELL YOURSELF 5 POSITIVE THINGS ABOUT YOU

YES, YOU STILL HAVE WORK TO DO, BUT IT'S SO WORTH IT. THE GOAL IS CONSISTENCY NOT TO BE PERFECT. WE WILL CONTINUE TO TAKE THIS ONE DAY AT A TIME.

THINK OF 5 WORDS YOU WOULD LIKE TO FOCUS ON FOR THIS WEEK..

WEEKLY Spotlight Words

Okay.... Let's see what did you decide. What are you focusing on today!

1 ....

2 ....

3 ....

4 ....

5 ....

Check "Y" for every day you focused on your spotlight words. Check "N" if you missed that day.

WEEKLY
Spotlight Accountability

You made it though this week. Let's check on your consistentcy !!!

Fill in one slice for every "Y" you had this week.

/ 5

THIS IS WEEK 1. CRUSH THIS ACTIVITY.

WEEKLY Spotlight Words

Okay…. Let's see what did you decide.
What are you focusing on today!

1 ....

2 ....

3 ....

4 ....

5 ....

Check "Y" for every day you focused on your spotlight words. Check "N" if you missed that day.

WEEKLY
Spotlight Accountability

You made it though this week. Let's check on your consistentcy !!!

Fill in one slice for every "Y" you had this week.

/ 5

YES! I'M SO PROUD OF YOU!

WEEKLY Spotlight Words

Okay.... Let's see what did you decide.
What are you focusing on today!

1 ....

2 ....

3 ....

4 ....

5 ....

Check "Y" for every day you focused on your spotlight words. Check "N" if you missed that day.

WEEKLY
Spotlight Accountability

You made it though this week. Let's check on your consistentcy !!!

Fill in one slice for every "Y" you had this week.

/ 5

KEEP GOING !

WEEKLY Spotlight Words

Okay.... Let's see what did you decide.
What are you focusing on today!

1 ....

2 ....

3 ....

4 ....

5 ....

Check "Y" for every day you focused on your spotlight words. Check "N" if you missed that day.

WEEKLY
Spotlight Accountability

You made it though this week.
Let's check on your consistentcy
!!!

Fill in one
slice for
every "Y" you
had this
week.

/ 5

WOW YOU ARE DOING AMAZING

Okay.... Let's see what did you decide.
What are you focusing on today!

1 ....

2 ....

3 ....

4 ....

5 ....

Check "Y" for every day you focused on your spotlight words. Check "N" if you missed that day.

You made it though this week.
Let's check on your consistentcy
!!!

Fill in one
slice for
every "Y" you
had this
week.

/ 5

DON'T STOP!

WEEKLY Spotlight Words

1 ....

2 ....

3 ....

4 ....

5 ....

Check "Y" for every day you focused on your spotlight words. Check "N" if you missed that day.

WEEKLY
Spotlight Accountability

You made it though this week.
Let's check on your consistentcy
!!!

Fill in one slice for every "Y" you had this week.

/ 5

YOU DID IT!!!!!

WEEKLY
Spotlight Accountability

I COULD JUST REACH OUT AND BEAR HUG YOU RIGHT NOW. YOU MIGHT LOVE YOUR RESULTS OR YOU MAY NOT. I AM SO HAPPY THAT YOU'RE HERE RIGHT NOW. YOU HAVEN'T GIVEN UP ON YOURSELF. TAKE A MOMENT TO CELEBRATE YOURSELF

WEEKLY
Spotlight Accountability

You made it though this week. Let's check on your consistentcy !!!

Tell me you reached 100%.
I would love to hear it, but if you fell short then that's okay.

Showing up means you did what you said. You showed up & that is something to celebrate.

LET'S PLAY A GAME!

CALLED...

Let's Catch That Thought

Did you learn how to tell good thoughts from negative thoughts? Let's find out .....

I got a bad grade on my math test. I wish I was smart like everyone else.
Negative or Positive
I am smart always. I will study harder and ask my teacher for help. I will do better next time, I don't have to do this alone.

Negative or Positive

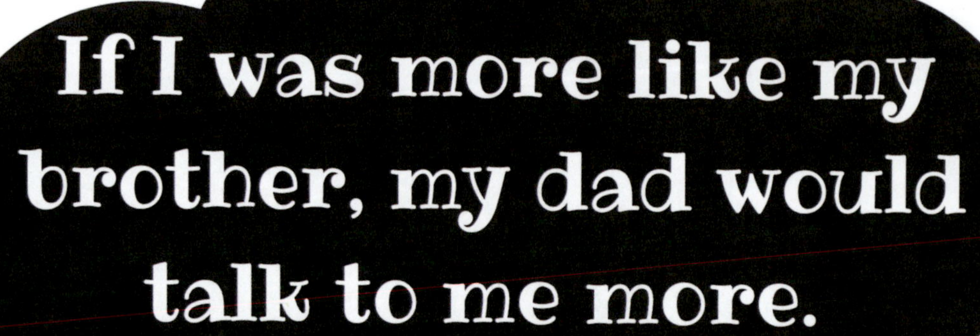

Negative or Positive

LET'S MIX

THINGS
UP ...

I am special
and loved.

Negative
or
Positive

I will
apologize to
those I hurt.

Negative
or
Positive

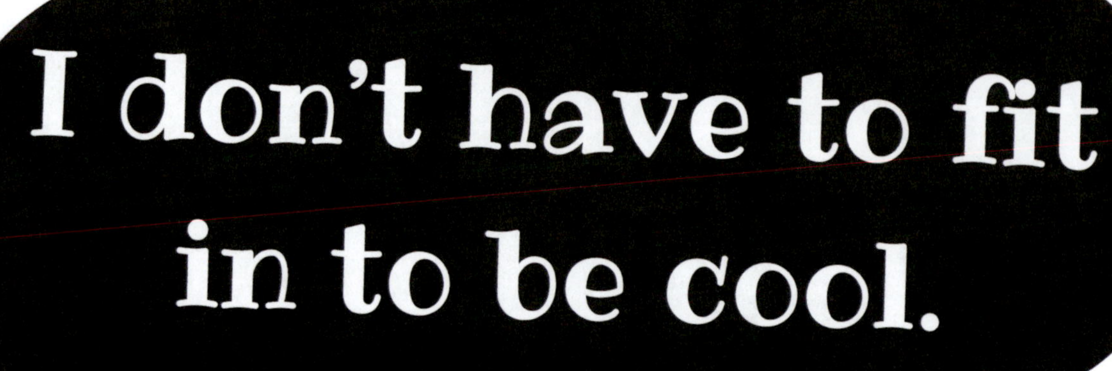

I don't have to fit in to be cool.

Negative
or
Positive

SO.....
HOW
EASY

WAS
THAT?

OKAY LET'S SEE... WAS THIS TIME TOGETHER WORTH IT?

Who are you?

You Did It!

You did it! You absolutely committed to the end, and I'm so proud of you. You didn't get it right 1000%, but no one does.Thank you so much for being obedient and deicated. You proved to yourself that you can change your reality.